I Wonder Why

Flutes Have Holes

and Other Questions About Music

Josephine Paker

Kingfisher

NEW YORK

KINGFISHER
Larousse Kingfisher Chambers Inc.
95 Madison Avenue
New York, New York 10016

First edition 1995
10 9 8 7 6 5 4 3 2 (HB)
10 9 8 7 6 5 4 3 2 1 (RLB)
Copyright © Larousse plc 1995
7-14-11   10·00
LIBRARY OF CONGRESS CATALOGING-IN-PUBLICATION DATA
Paker, Josephine.
    I wonder why flutes have holes and other questions about
    music/by Josephine Paker.
    1st American ed.
        p.   cm.
    Includes index.
    1. Music — Miscellanea — Juvenile literature.
    [1. Music — Miscellanea. 2. Questions and answers.]
I. Title. II. Series: I wonder why (New York, N.Y.)
    ML3928. P35 1995 94-45002 CIP AC MN

ISBN 1-85697-583-5 (HB)
ISBN 1-85697-640-8 (RLB)
Printed in Italy

Series editor: Clare Oliver
Series designer: David West Children's Books
Consultant: Peter Thoms
Thanks to: Waseda University, Tokyo
Illustrations: Peter Dennis (Linda Rogers); Diane Fawcett
(Artist Partners); Chris Forsey; Nick Harris (Virgil
Pomfret); Biz Hull (Artist Partners) cover;
Tony Kenyon (B.L. Kearley) all cartoons; Nicki Palin;
Richard Ward; David Wright
(Kathy Jakeman).

CONTENTS

How do you sing a round?

A round is a song for two or more singers. Everyone sings the same tune, but they start singing at different times. When the first singer finishes the first line, the second singer starts, and so on. One of the best-known rounds is called *Frère Jacques*.

• A round gets louder and louder as each singer joins in, and softer and softer as everyone finishes their part.

• Singing can help you to learn things—your multiplication tables, for instance. Singing makes them much easier to remember.

• People sing *Happy Birthday to You* more than any other song in the world. At first it wasn't a birthday song at all. It was called *Good Morning to All*.

4

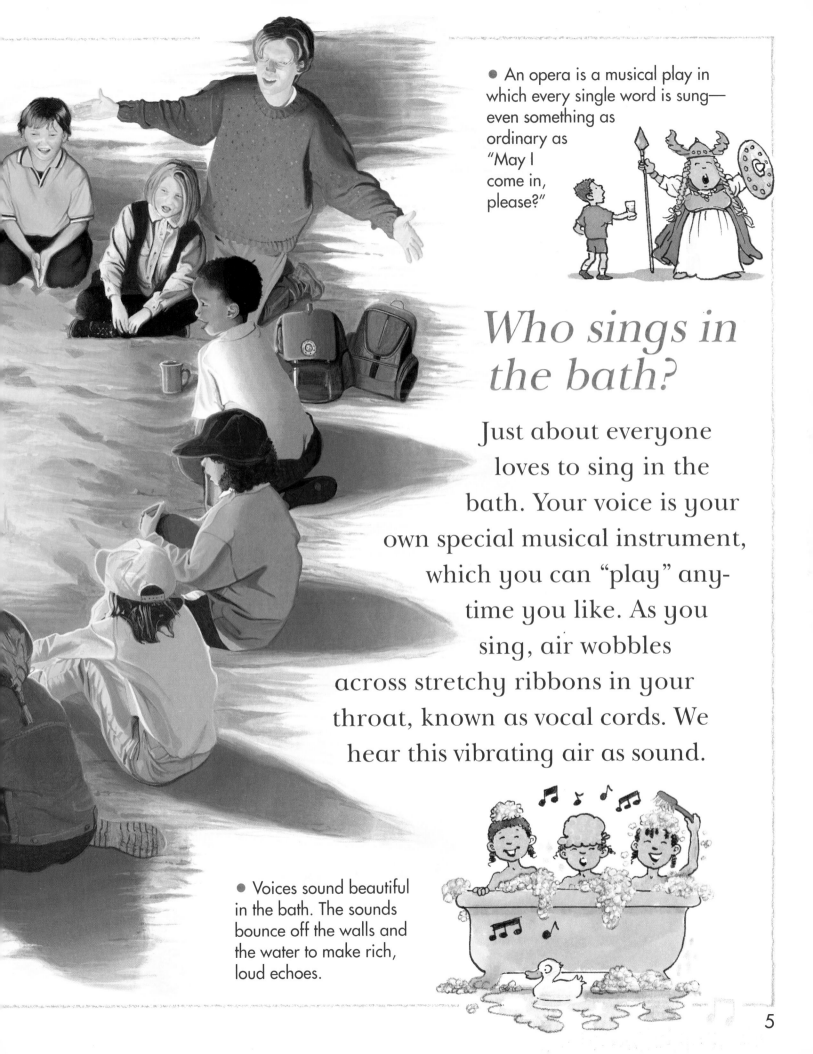

● An opera is a musical play in which every single word is sung—even something as ordinary as "May I come in, please?"

Who sings in the bath?

Just about everyone loves to sing in the bath. Your voice is your own special musical instrument, which you can "play" anytime you like. As you sing, air wobbles across stretchy ribbons in your throat, known as vocal cords. We hear this vibrating air as sound.

● Voices sound beautiful in the bath. The sounds bounce off the walls and the water to make rich, loud echoes.

How do marching bands keep time?

Left, right, left, right! As a band marches along, the players move their feet in time to the music. The big bass drum booms out the beat to keep the band in step.

• The majorette leads the parade. She has a stick, called a baton, which she twirls and tosses high in the air as she marches along.

How fast is fast?

So you know how fast a piece of music should be, the composer tells you how many beats it has in every minute. To copy this speed, you use a metronome. Just set this machine ticking and play in time with its ticks.

● When you listen to music, it's often hard not to join in! Your toes tap and your hands clap to the music's rhythmic beat.

● Your heart beats about 90 times every minute, but you may find it speeds up when you're listening to fast, exciting music.

● Have you heard the song 1,000 ? It has 1,000 beats every minute. It's so fast that you can't hear separate notes —they all smudge together!

Who worked to the beat?

Oarsmen on Greek warships worked in time to the music of a drummer or piper. The beat kept the oars moving smoothly together through the water.

Where can you play an oil drum?

In the Caribbean islands, large empty oil drums are made into musical drums called steel drums. The top is hammered into a curved dish-shape. This metal dish is then beaten and "tuned" until the different parts of the steel drum make a number of musical sounds. Some drums can play 30 different notes.

● Steel bands play outside in the streets or on the beach at carnival time.

Who bangs on the bongos?

A drummer in a South American dance band often plays the bongos. He grips the drums between his knees and taps them with his fingers and the palm of his hand. This makes zippy rhythms that soon get you dancing.

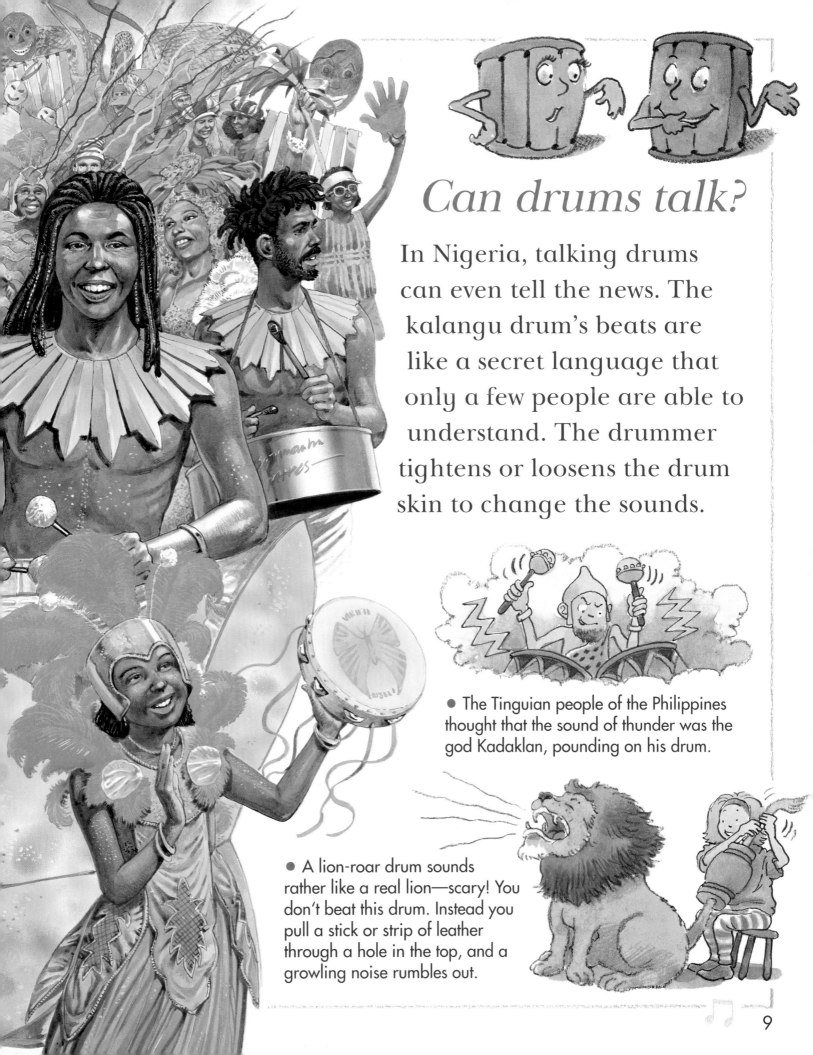

Can drums talk?

In Nigeria, talking drums can even tell the news. The kalangu drum's beats are like a secret language that only a few people are able to understand. The drummer tightens or loosens the drum skin to change the sounds.

● The Tinguian people of the Philippines thought that the sound of thunder was the god Kadaklan, pounding on his drum.

● A lion-roar drum sounds rather like a real lion—scary! You don't beat this drum. Instead you pull a stick or strip of leather through a hole in the top, and a growling noise rumbles out.

Where can you find a gamelan?

A gamelan is a kind of orchestra from Indonesia. Drums, gongs, xylophones, and chimes all play together to make a magical tinkling sound. There can be as many as 40 instruments in a gamelan.

● Gamelan players treat their instruments with great respect.

● Washboards are just trays to scrub clothes on. But some jazz musicians play them like an instrument. They scrape a stick or thimble across the ridges.

Are rattles just for babies?

Babies aren't the only ones who like the dry, swishing sound rattles make. The first ones were probably dried plant pods, full of seeds. South American rattles called maracas are still often filled with dried beans. You could fill a yogurt tub with some to make your own rattle.

● The triangle is one of the smallest instruments. Larger triangles are used to warn people about fire in some parts of the world, but sirens work better on noisy roads!

What roars like a bull?

The bull-roarer doesn't really roar like an angry bull! It's a block of wood fixed to a piece of string. You whirl it above your head and it makes a strange screaming noise.

Are guitar strings really made of string?

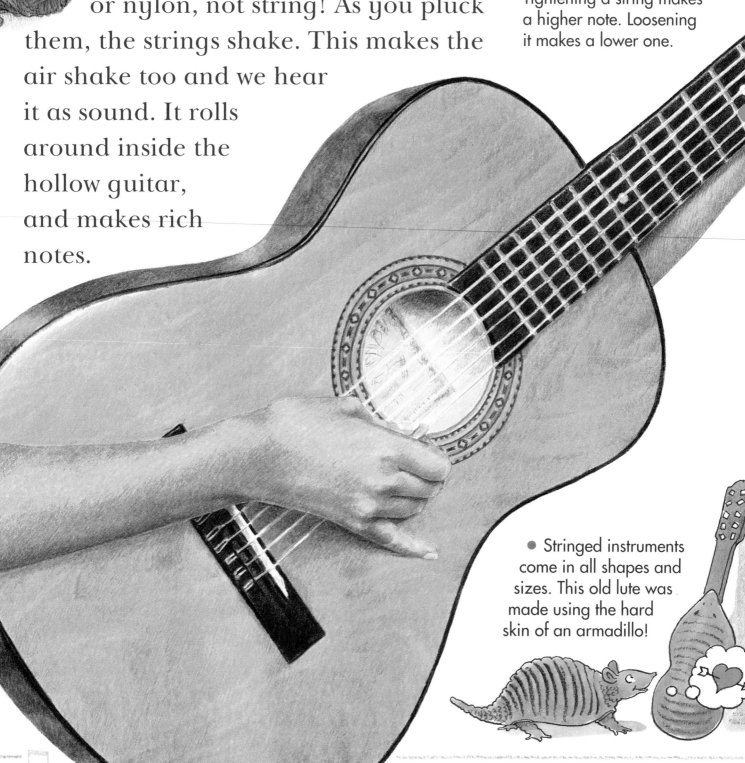

Like all musical strings, guitar strings are usually made of metal or nylon, not string! As you pluck them, the strings shake. This makes the air shake too and we hear it as sound. It rolls around inside the hollow guitar, and makes rich notes.

● You tune a stringed instrument by turning the pegs at the end of its neck. Tightening a string makes a higher note. Loosening it makes a lower one.

● Stringed instruments come in all shapes and sizes. This old lute was made using the hard skin of an armadillo!

What's double about a double bass?

The double bass got its name because it used to "double," or copy, the cello. "Bass" means low, and the double bass *does* have a deep voice! Pluck one of its thick strings and it makes a very low note.

● Niccolo Paganini was a genius on the violin. He could play it behind his back, upside-down, and with a blindfold on!

How do you learn the sitar?

The sitar (**sit**-ar) is one of the most difficult stringed instruments to play. To learn it, you have to watch and listen to a skilled player. Players learn groups of notes called ragas, and then put them together to make beautiful, haunting music.

● The Indian vina balances comfortably on the shoulder as the player plucks the strings.

Why do flutes have holes?

To play the flute, you blow over the blowhole. The air shakes its way down the tube and you hear it come out as a musical sound. You change notes by covering and uncovering the different holes in the flute with your fingers.

● Pennywhistles belong to the same family of musical instruments as flutes—the woodwind family. You play the pennywhistle like a recorder, by blowing into the mouth-piece, and covering the holes.

● Panpipes are named after an ancient Greek god called Pan, who was half goat. He cut some reeds of different lengths, tied them together, and blew across the top.

When is a serpent not a serpent?

When it's a woodwind instrument! It's easy to see how the serpent got its snaky name—it's so curly! It was invented 400 years ago, but isn't played much these days.

● Snakes are deaf, but they sway in time to a snake-charmer's music. They keep their eyes on the pipe, in case it's an enemy snake!

● In Tibet you sometimes hear monks playing a long, straight trumpet. It's so heavy that the far end has to be held up as the monk plays.

How do you stretch brass?

The trombone is one brass instrument that needs stretching. It has a long, sliding arm. The trombonist moves this slide in and out to make the different notes.

15

Who sits where in an orchestra?

The players in an orchestra all have their own place to sit. This depends on which instrument they play, and which "family" the instrument belongs to. Violins, cellos, and other stringed instruments all sit together at the front and the noisier brass and woodwind instruments are at the back.

● Johann Strauss conducted a vast orchestra in 1872. There were nearly 1,000 players, with over 400 people playing the violin.

● The French composer Jean-Baptiste Lully used to conduct by banging a big stick on the floor. One day, he missed and banged his own foot instead! Ouch!

Drums

Piano

French horns

Harp

Clarinets

Percussion

Tuba

Trombones

Bassoon

Double basses

Trumpets

Oboes

Cellos

Flutes

Violins

● The conductor is the boss.
He or she tells the musicians
when to play, how loudly to
play, how fast, and—of
course—when to stop!

Who writes music?

People who write music are called composers. They write down musical notes just as you write down words. Music isn't always written down though. Some people learn how to play a piece of music by simply copying a teacher or something they have heard.

● Many composers don't write down their ideas on paper anymore. They key in the notes on a computer and can immediately play back what they have written.

Which five-year-old composed music?

Wolfgang Amadeus Mozart was a musical genius. At five, he composed his very first piece of music. By the time he died, aged only thirty-five, he had written more than 600 works.

● Mozart was one of the greatest—and youngest—composers. His father took him on a tour of Europe to show him off.

Which composer was deaf?

The German composer Ludwig van Beethoven slowly became deaf. At first he used a curly ear trumpet to help him to hear, but it was no use. Soon he was composing music in his head that he was never able to hear.

● Musical notes are written on a set of five lines called a stave. A high note is written high up on the stave. The shape of the note, and whether it's black or white, shows how long it should last.

● Music isn't always written down. Jazz musicians often make up the music as they go along. This is called "improvisation."

Which is the biggest instrument?

The organ is the biggest musical instrument. Organ music can make the windows rattle! The largest and loudest organ in the world is in Atlantic City, New Jersey. It's so huge that it sounds as loud as 25 brass bands playing together! It has 12 keyboards and over 33,000 pipes. Sadly, this record-breaking instrument doesn't work very well these days.

● The Russian composer Sergei Rachmaninov had enormous hands. Each hand could stretch over 12 keys on the piano—that's probably twice as far as you could manage.

What's the longest piece of music ever played?

It takes all day and half the night to listen to a performance of Erik Satie's *Vexations*. This is because the piece has to be played 840 times. It needs six pianists to take turns with the playing. Just one might fall asleep!

● This enormous guitar in Bristol, England, is so huge that you can climb inside it. If you twang its strings the noise is deafening!

Which is the most valuable instrument?

Three hundred years ago, an Italian called Antonio Stradivari made the most wonderful violins. His instruments are now so rare and so valuable that they cost a fortune— far more than the price of a house!

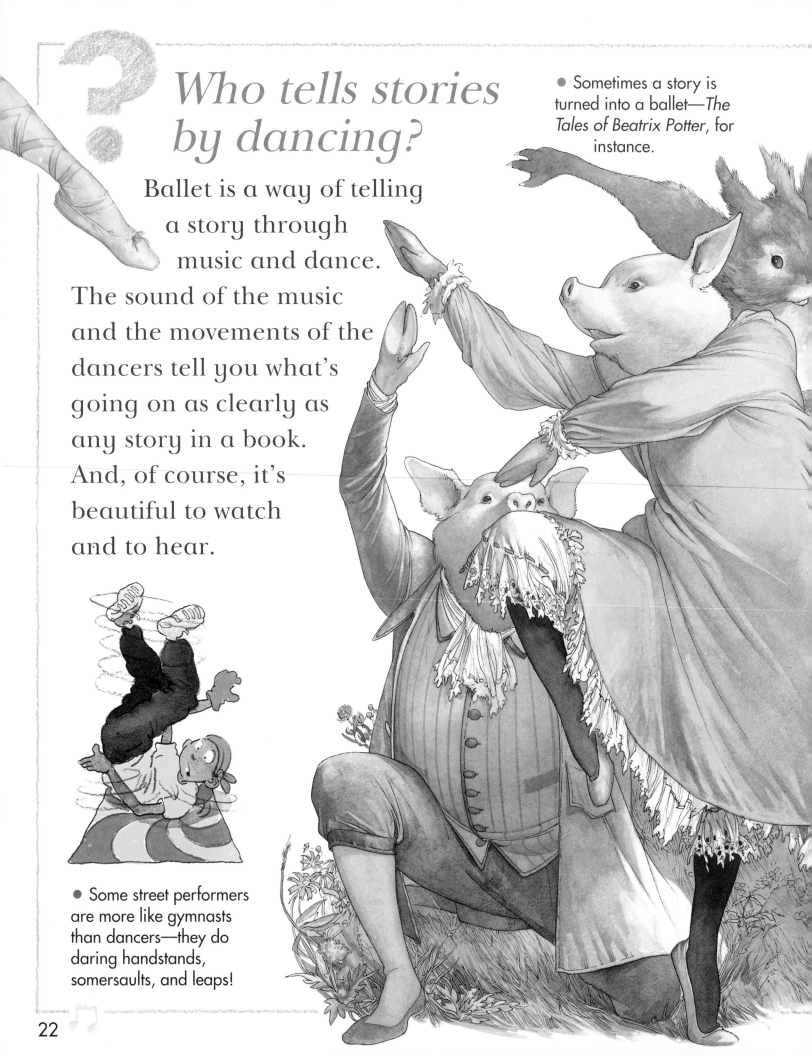

Who tells stories by dancing?

Ballet is a way of telling a story through music and dance. The sound of the music and the movements of the dancers tell you what's going on as clearly as any story in a book. And, of course, it's beautiful to watch and to hear.

● Sometimes a story is turned into a ballet—*The Tales of Beatrix Potter*, for instance.

● Some street performers are more like gymnasts than dancers—they do daring handstands, somersaults, and leaps!

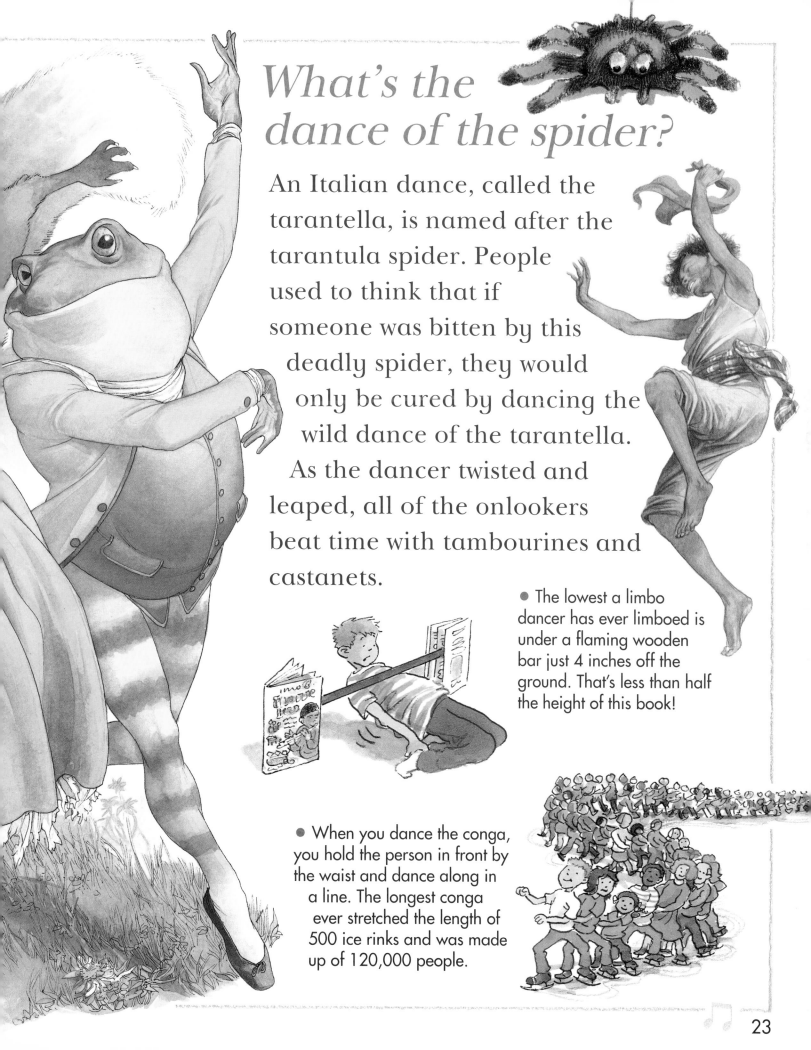

What's the dance of the spider?

An Italian dance, called the tarantella, is named after the tarantula spider. People used to think that if someone was bitten by this deadly spider, they would only be cured by dancing the wild dance of the tarantella. As the dancer twisted and leaped, all of the onlookers beat time with tambourines and castanets.

● The lowest a limbo dancer has ever limboed is under a flaming wooden bar just 4 inches off the ground. That's less than half the height of this book!

● When you dance the conga, you hold the person in front by the waist and dance along in a line. The longest conga ever stretched the length of 500 ice rinks and was made up of 120,000 people.

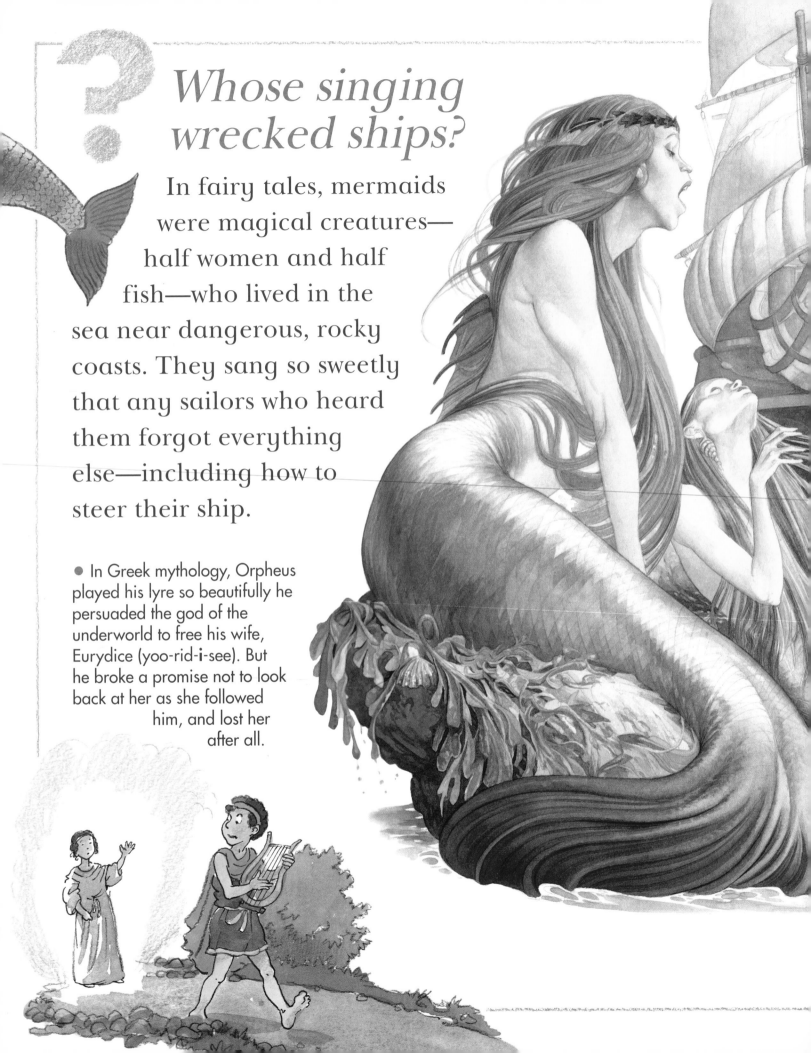

Whose singing wrecked ships?

In fairy tales, mermaids were magical creatures—half women and half fish—who lived in the sea near dangerous, rocky coasts. They sang so sweetly that any sailors who heard them forgot everything else—including how to steer their ship.

● In Greek mythology, Orpheus played his lyre so beautifully he persuaded the god of the underworld to free his wife, Eurydice (yoo-rid-i-see). But he broke a promise not to look back at her as she followed him, and lost her after all.

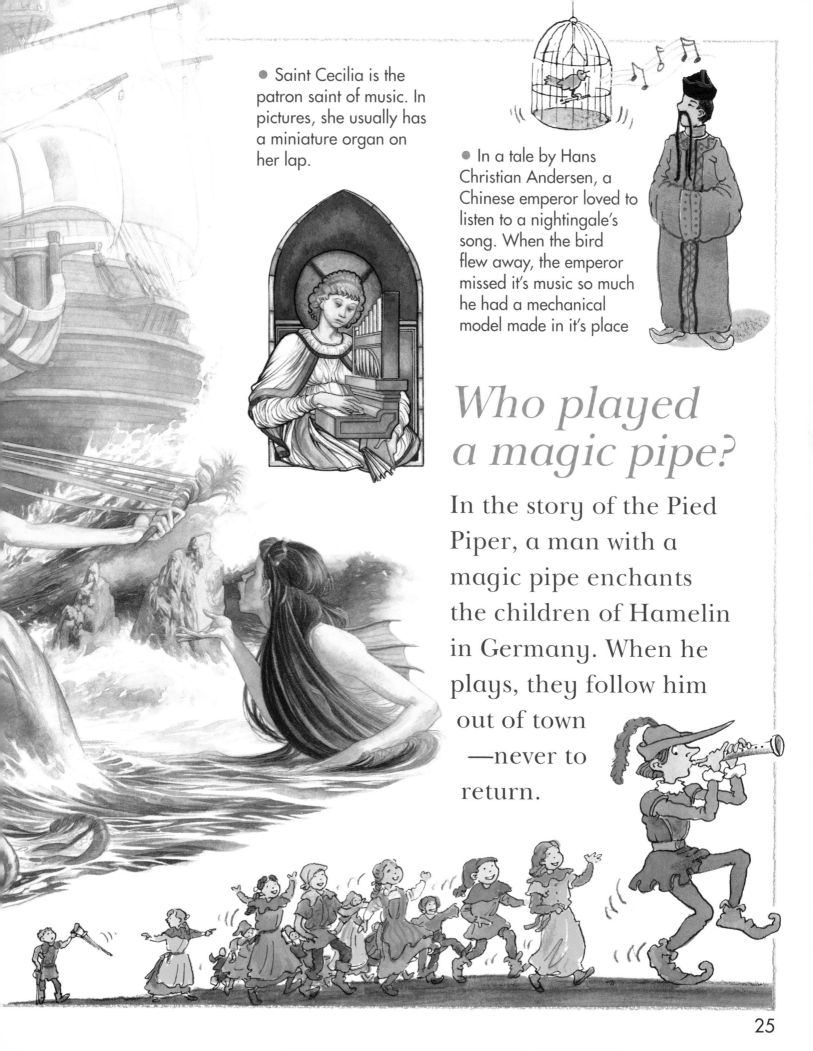

● Saint Cecilia is the patron saint of music. In pictures, she usually has a miniature organ on her lap.

● In a tale by Hans Christian Andersen, a Chinese emperor loved to listen to a nightingale's song. When the bird flew away, the emperor missed it's music so much he had a mechanical model made in it's place

Who played a magic pipe?

In the story of the Pied Piper, a man with a magic pipe enchants the children of Hamelin in Germany. When he plays, they follow him out of town —never to return.

Which frog sings?

Male frogs love to sing. They puff out their throats to make a big space where the air can vibrate and the concert begins. Frogs sing surprisingly loudly, but it's not everyone's idea of music!

● The composer Domenico Scarlatti wrote a piece that is nicknamed *Cat's Fugue*. Scarlatti said that his cat made up the tune as it tiptoed along the keys of his harpsichord!

Which mouse is musical?

The male grasshopper mouse of North America uses his shrill, chirping song to attract a mate. He stands up on his back legs and sings his heart out. It's his way of telling all the female mice around what a fine, strong mouse he is.

Who sings the dawn chorus?

As the Sun rises on spring and summer mornings, the birds wake up and start to twitter. This makes a beautiful dawn chorus. Some songs warn other birds to keep away. Some tell a mate where to find some tasty food.

● Each bird has its own special song, unlike any other's. Birds recognize each other by their song, just as we recognize a friend by their voice.

Who sings under water?

Humpback whales seem to sing to each other under the ocean. Some scientists think the whales are singing about where they've swum and what they've been doing. No other animal's song lasts as long as the humpback whale's, and it can be heard hundreds of miles away.

● Elephants sometimes use their trunks like a musical instrument. They blow through them and make a tremendous trumpeting noise.

How do termites help to make music?

The didgeridoo (dij-uh-ree-**doo**) is a long musical pipe from Australia made from a log of the eucalyptus tree, which is buried inside a termites' mound. The termites gnaw away at the soft wood inside the log, leaving a hollow pipe. Then the pipe is decorated. Didgeridoos can be hollowed out by hand, but they don't give the same rich sound.

Which harp fits inside your mouth?

The tiny Jew's harp doesn't look like its larger cousin. You put it between your teeth, and twang its metal tongue with your finger. It makes your lips feel funny because the metal vibrates so much.

● Didgeridoo-players can breathe in at the same time as they're blowing out through their instrument.

● The Masai people of Kenya play an instrument called a thumb piano. It has metal strips which you pluck with your thumb.

Which instrument is made with a spiderweb?

Take a cow's horn, make a little hole at the pointed end, cover the wide end with a tough kind of spiderweb, and you have a mirliton (**mur**-lee-ton). These are played in Africa. They make a buzzy sound when you blow or sing through them.

● A jazz musician called Roland Kirk could play three saxophones at once! He must have had big lungs!

● Not all bagpipes come from Scotland. This African goatskin bagpipe has been decorated with a carved wooden goat's head!

Can a robot play the piano?

A clever Japanese robot called WABOT-2 can whizz its fingers over a keyboard much faster than a human can. It can either read new music, or choose a song it has played before and stored in its memory. The cleverest thing about WABOT-2 is its sensitive fingers. It can play gently or furiously.

● WABOT-2's head is like a camcorder. As the robot reads music, the camera "films" what it sees and stores it in its memory to play again.

WABOT-2

Where do people mix music?

In a recording studio, the voices and instruments are recorded separately. The producer mixes the parts together on a machine called a mixing desk. He or she checks the sounds are balanced and every part can be heard clearly.

- Drum machines make the sound of all kinds of drums—but they're only as big as a candy box. Some of them have pads to tap out the rhythm on.

- You can record any sound you like on a sampler —even a dog's bark. You put the sounds you've sampled into tunes as if they were musical notes.

Can you be an entire orchestra?

Synthesizers are machines that can make the sound of every instrument in the orchestra. One minute they sound like a flute, the next they sound like a violin. They'll even play a simple drum pattern to give your music a beat.

Index